INTRODUCTION

It is no surprise to anyone that Daddy is special, especially to his children.
Where Mom makes you behave in public, often you will find Dad
teasing his child at the table by blowing water through a straw.
Where Mom makes you sit up, use your manners and say, "Please,"
you will often find Dad on the scene, agreeing with her verbally,
but poking you with a wet lettuce leaf under the table.

Camille and her friends at BBC Academy tell you how they feel about their dads.
As you read the words that are literally "out of the mouths of babes",
perhaps you will remember all the fun you used to have with your dad.
I helped my daughter Camille put this book together, but the research was all hers.
Thank you Camille, and thank you, BBCA students.

Laura Mauk

Daddy & Me

WHAT IS THE MOST IMPORTANT THING
YOUR FATHER HAS TAUGHT YOU?

My father taught me to work hard.

Joey
Age 7

School-aged children were asked to tell what they love about their fathers in this fun and tender collection.

Cover Illustration by MarketForce
Typography by MarketForce

Published by Great Quotations Publishing Co.,
Glendale Heights, IL

Library of Congress Catalog Card Number: 97-071650

ISBN 1-56245-312-2

Printed in Hong Kong

Daddy & Me

WHAT IS THE MOST IMPORTANT THING
YOUR FATHER HAS TAUGHT YOU?

**My dad taught me to ride my bike
and to love God and read the Bible.**

Mary
Age 5

Daddy & Me

WHAT IS THE MOST IMPORTANT THING
YOUR FATHER HAS TAUGHT YOU?

My father taught me not to lie.

Aaron

Age 10

Daddy & Me

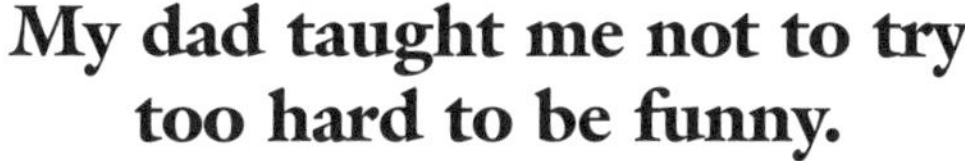

My dad taught me not to try too hard to be funny.

Pat

Age 9

Daddy & Me

WHAT IS THE MOST IMPORTANT THING
YOUR FATHER HAS TAUGHT YOU?

**My father taught me
that I shouldn't say bad words.**

Jenny
Age 5

Daddy & Me

WHAT IS THE MOST IMPORTANT THING
YOUR FATHER HAS TAUGHT YOU?

**I shouldn't do something
just because everyone else is.**

Tim
Age 11

Daddy & Me

WHAT IS THE MOST IMPORTANT THING
YOUR FATHER HAS TAUGHT YOU?

My father taught me that I am to obey him.

Joey
Age 6

WHAT IS THE MOST IMPORTANT THING
YOUR FATHER HAS TAUGHT YOU?

**My father taught me
to respect other people's property.**

Rachelle

Age 6

Daddy & Me

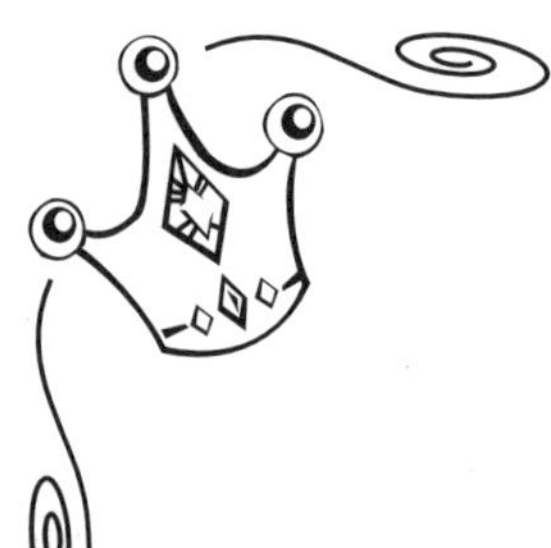

WHAT IS THE MOST IMPORTANT THING
YOUR FATHER HAS TAUGHT YOU?

**My father taught me
to take care of my, or someone else's, property.**

Ginger

Age 11

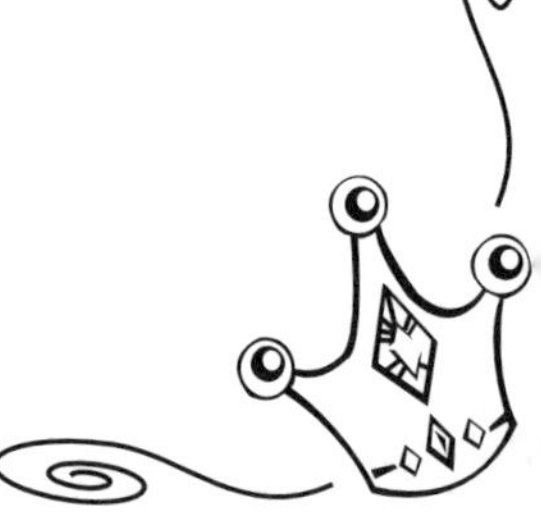

Daddy & Me

WHAT IS THE MOST IMPORTANT THING
YOUR FATHER HAS TAUGHT YOU?

My father taught me to always do my best.

Melissa

Age 12

Daddy & Me

WHAT IS THE MOST IMPORTANT THING
YOUR FATHER HAS TAUGHT YOU?

**My father taught me
that I should not run in the house!**

Vicki

Age 6

Daddy & Me

WHAT IS THE MOST IMPORTANT THING
YOUR FATHER HAS TAUGHT YOU?

My dad taught me not to be mean.

April

Age 12

Daddy & Me

WHAT IS THE MOST IMPORTANT THING
YOUR FATHER HAS TAUGHT YOU?

My dad taught me to be kind to one another.

Nicole

Age 5

Daddy & Me

**My dad said I should never smoke because
he used to and he said it is bad for your health.**

Dave

Age 13

Daddy & Me

WHAT IS THE MOST IMPORTANT THING
YOUR FATHER HAS TAUGHT YOU?

My father taught me to believe and trust in God.

Sean

Age 8 ½

Daddy & Me

WHAT IS THE MOST IMPORTANT THING
YOUR FATHER HAS TAUGHT YOU?

The most important lesson my dad taught me was vegetables.

Mikaela

Age 2 ½

Daddy & Me

WHAT IS THE MOST IMPORTANT THING
YOUR FATHER HAS TAUGHT YOU?

If I study I will be real smart.

Jan

Age 8

Daddy & Me

WHAT IS THE MOST ENJOYABLE THING
YOU AND YOUR DAD LIKE TO DO TOGETHER?

**We have food fights when
we go to restaurants.**

Camille

Age 12

Daddy & Me

WHAT IS THE MOST ENJOYABLE THING
YOU AND YOUR DAD LIKE TO DO TOGETHER?

I like going shopping with my dad.

Joey G.

Age 7

Daddy & Me

WHAT IS THE MOST ENJOYABLE THING
YOU AND YOUR DAD LIKE TO DO TOGETHER?

**I like to go out on a date
for breakfast with Daddy.**

Mary

Age 5

Daddy & Me

WHAT IS THE MOST ENJOYABLE THING
YOU AND YOUR DAD LIKE TO DO TOGETHER?

Me and my dad get to dig holes to fix the pipes.

Marshall

Age 6

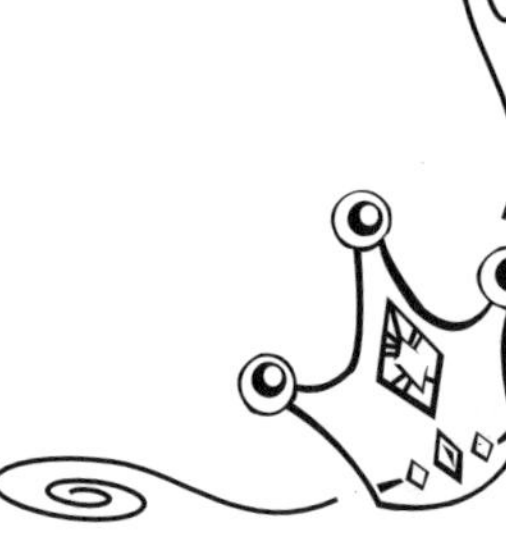

Daddy & Me

**Dad and I like to launch
our toy rocket together!**

Aaron

Age 10

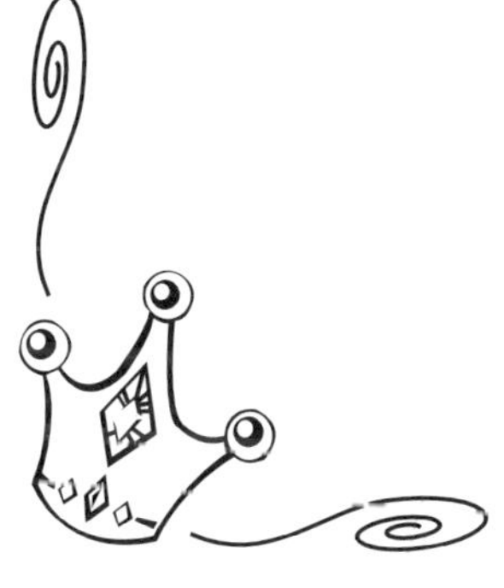

Daddy & Me

WHAT IS THE MOST ENJOYABLE THING
YOU AND YOUR DAD LIKE TO DO TOGETHER?

**We get to work with him
in his office on Saturdays.**

Mark

Age 7

Daddy & Me

WHAT IS THE MOST ENJOYABLE THING
YOU AND YOUR DAD LIKE TO DO TOGETHER?

**I like to go to Indian Princess
with my daddy.**

Molly

Age 6

Daddy & Me

WHAT IS THE MOST ENJOYABLE THING
YOU AND YOUR DAD LIKE TO DO TOGETHER?

I like to play games with my dad.

Jenny
Age 5

Daddy & Me

WHAT IS THE MOST ENJOYABLE THING
YOU AND YOUR DAD LIKE TO DO TOGETHER?

I like to ride horsy-back on daddy.

Rachelle

Age 6

Daddy & Me

WHAT IS THE MOST ENJOYABLE THING
YOU AND YOUR DAD LIKE TO DO TOGETHER?

My dad and I like to wrestle.

Ginger

Age 11

Daddy & Me

WHAT IS THE MOST ENJOYABLE THING
YOU AND YOUR DAD LIKE TO DO TOGETHER?

**We like to get ice cream
and go to the zoo or to the museum.**

Melissa

Age 12

Daddy & Me

**I like to play with my dad,
to jump on him.**

Vicki

Age 6

Daddy & Me

WHAT IS THE MOST ENJOYABLE THING
YOU AND YOUR DAD LIKE TO DO TOGETHER?

**I like to have pillow fights
with my daddy.**

Nicole

Age 5

Daddy & Me

WHAT IS THE MOST ENJOYABLE THING
YOU AND YOUR DAD LIKE TO DO TOGETHER?

My dad and I like to fish.

Dave

Age 13

Daddy & Me

WHAT IS THE MOST ENJOYABLE THING
YOU AND YOUR DAD LIKE TO DO TOGETHER?

My dad and I like to watch TV together.

Sean

Age 8 ½

Daddy & Me

WHAT IS THE MOST ENJOYABLE THING
YOU AND YOUR DAD LIKE TO DO TOGETHER?

I like to play telephone with my dad.

Mikaela

Age 2 ½

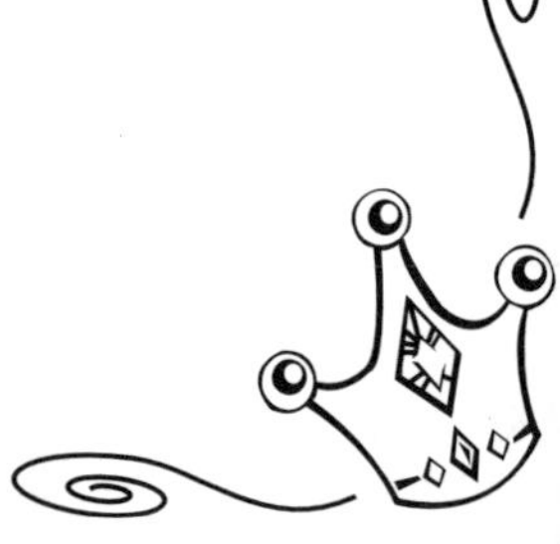

Daddy & Me

WHAT IS THE MOST ENJOYABLE THING
YOU AND YOUR DAD LIKE TO DO TOGETHER?

**The most enjoyable thing
my dad and I like to do is go to the show.**

April

Age 12

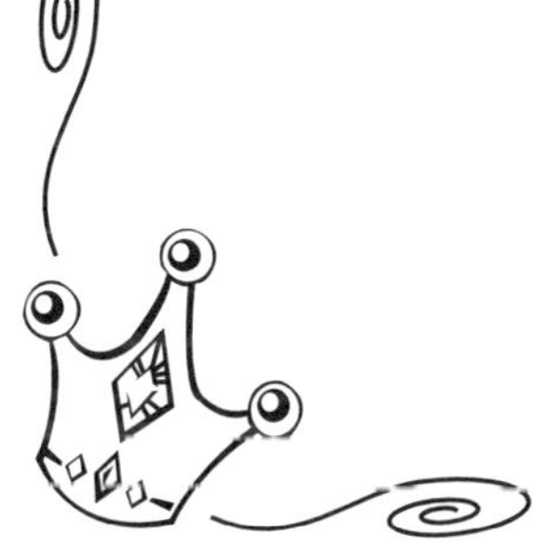

Daddy & Me

WHAT IS THE MOST ENJOYABLE THING
YOU AND YOUR DAD LIKE TO DO TOGETHER?

**-when daddy tickles me
and we wrestle on the waterbed.**

Joey

Age 6

Daddy & Me

WHAT IS THE MOST ENJOYABLE THING
YOU AND YOUR DAD LIKE TO DO TOGETHER?

We go for ice cream.

Jan

Age 8

Daddy & Me

IN WHAT WAYS WOULD YOU LIKE TO BE LIKE YOUR DAD?

I would like to work at ComEd, like my dad.

Joey
Age 7

Daddy & Me

IN WHAT WAYS WOULD YOU LIKE TO BE LIKE YOUR DAD?

I would like to be like my dad because he is nice and is always kind.

Jamie

Age 10

Daddy & Me

IN WHAT WAYS WOULD YOU LIKE TO BE LIKE YOUR DAD?

**I would like to be like my dad,
he loves God.**

Mary

Age 5

Daddy & Me

IN WHAT WAYS WOULD YOU LIKE TO BE LIKE YOUR DAD?

**I want to be like my dad
because he is nice and friendly.**

Jessica

Age 10

Daddy & Me

**I want to be like my dad
because he is very athletic.**

Vanessa

Age 10

44

Daddy & Me

IN WHAT WAYS WOULD YOU LIKE TO BE LIKE YOUR DAD?

My dad gets to use the riding lawnmower.

Joe

Age 8

Daddy & Me

IN WHAT WAYS WOULD YOU LIKE TO BE LIKE YOUR DAD?

**My dad is always thoughtful.
I want to be like that.**

Aaron

Age 10

Daddy & Me

IN WHAT WAYS WOULD YOU LIKE TO BE LIKE YOUR DAD?

**I want to use the computer,
like my dad.**

Jenny

Age 5

Daddy & Me

IN WHAT WAYS WOULD YOU LIKE TO BE LIKE YOUR DAD?

I want to be like my father because he is "hansum" and kind.

Jacque

Age 10

Daddy & Me

I would like to be as smart as my dad.

Rachelle

Age 6

Daddy & Me

IN WHAT WAYS WOULD YOU LIKE TO BE LIKE YOUR DAD?

**My dad is a vice president
and I want to be just like him.**

Nick

Age 10

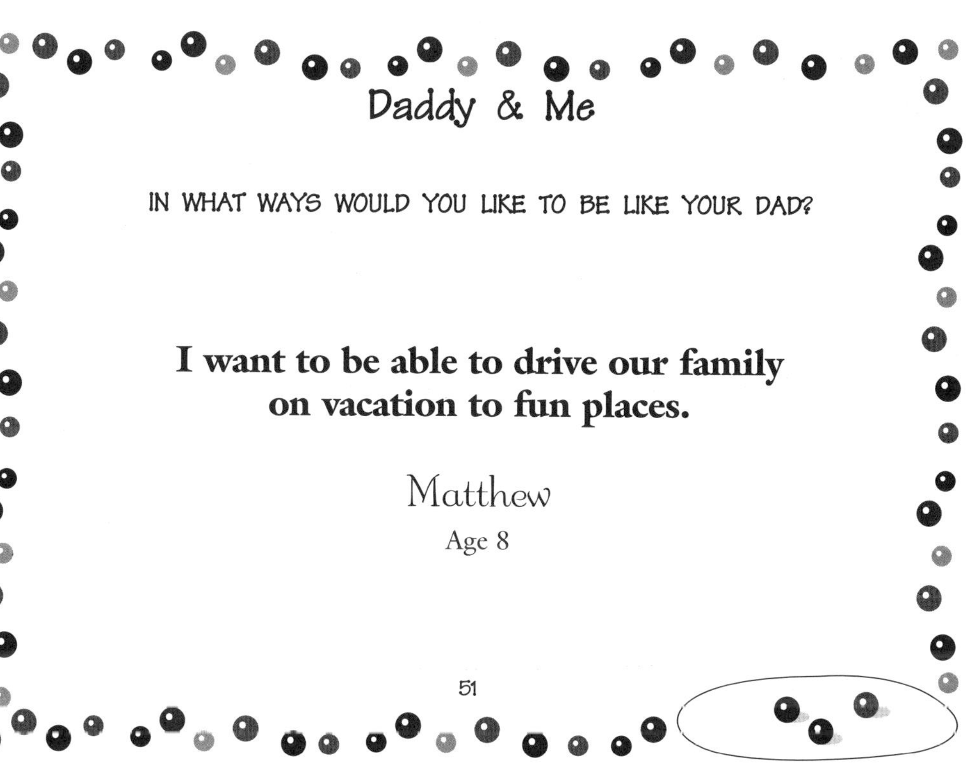

Daddy & Me

I want to be able to drive our family on vacation to fun places.

Matthew

Age 8

Daddy & Me

IN WHAT WAYS WOULD YOU LIKE TO BE LIKE YOUR DAD?

I want to patient, just like my dad.

Ginger

Age 11

Daddy & Me

IN WHAT WAYS WOULD YOU LIKE TO BE LIKE YOUR DAD?

I would like to be like my father because he is very smart.

Dan

Age 10

Daddy & Me

IN WHAT WAYS WOULD YOU LIKE TO BE LIKE YOUR DAD?

He is never mean to me and he likes to do things with me.

Joe

Age 8

Daddy & Me

IN WHAT WAYS WOULD YOU LIKE TO BE LIKE YOUR DAD?

I would like to be as funny as my dad is.

Melissa

Age 12

Daddy & Me

**I would like to be reliable like my dad.
When he says he is going to do
something he does it.**

Jamie

Age 10

Daddy & Me

IN WHAT WAYS WOULD YOU LIKE TO BE LIKE YOUR DAD?

I want to be like my father because he can chop wood for our fireplace.

Tim

Age 11

Daddy & Me

I want to fix things, like my dad, just to work like him.

Vicki

Age 6

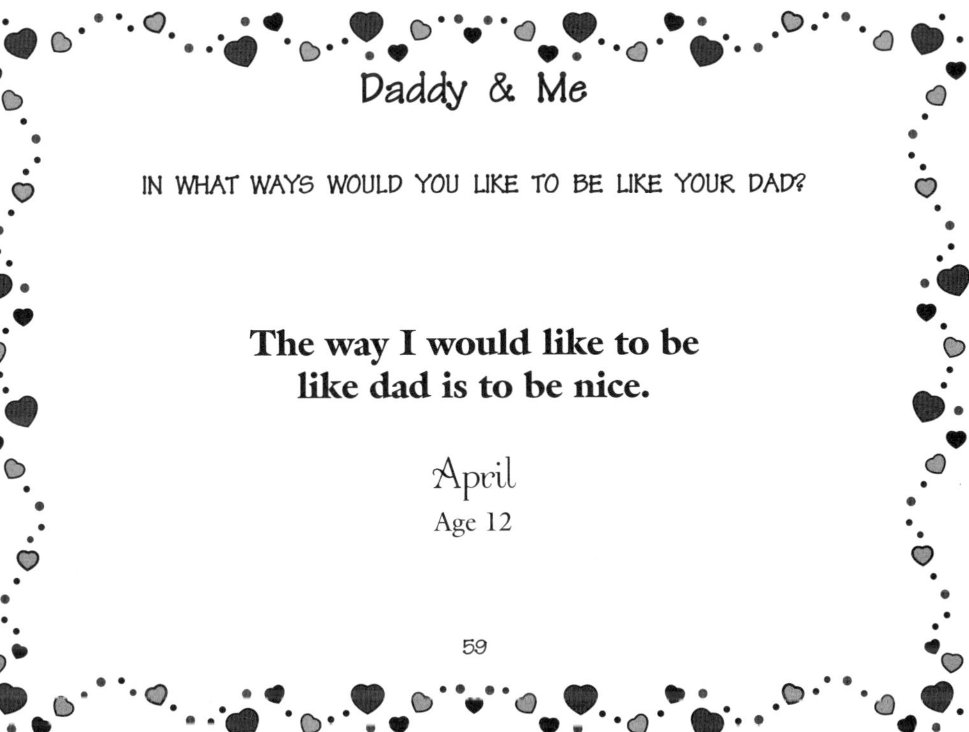

IN WHAT WAYS WOULD YOU LIKE TO BE LIKE YOUR DAD?

The way I would like to be like dad is to be nice.

April

Age 12

Daddy & Me

IN WHAT WAYS WOULD YOU LIKE TO BE LIKE YOUR DAD?

My dad is very fun. I want to be like him.

Kelly
Age 10

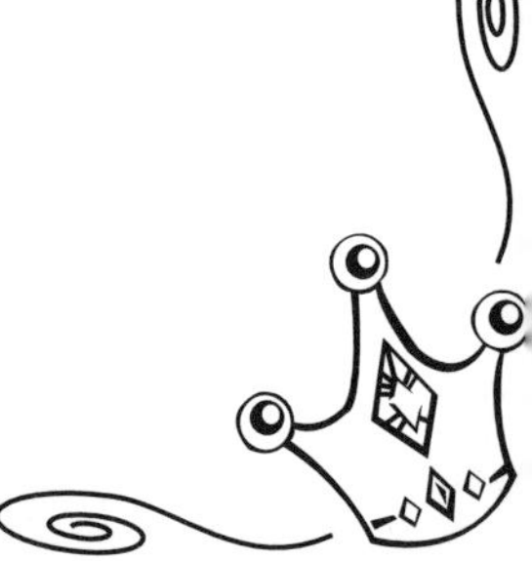

Daddy & Me

I'd like to be tall and skinny, like my dad.

Nicole

Age 5

Daddy & Me

IN WHAT WAYS WOULD YOU LIKE TO BE LIKE YOUR DAD?

I would like to be smart, like my dad.

Lori

Age 10

Daddy & Me

IN WHAT WAYS WOULD YOU LIKE TO BE LIKE YOUR DAD?

My dad works so hard to keep our family on their feet and I want to be like that.

Dave

Age 13

Daddy & Me

IN WHAT WAYS WOULD YOU LIKE TO BE LIKE YOUR DAD?

**I want to be like my dad because
I would spend time with my kids.**

Caitlin

Age 10

Daddy & Me

IN WHAT WAYS WOULD YOU LIKE TO BE LIKE YOUR DAD?

**My dad is a good dad.
I want to be a good dad some day.**

Sean

Age 8 ½

Daddy & Me

IN WHAT WAYS WOULD YOU LIKE TO BE LIKE YOUR DAD?

**I want to be like my dad because
he gets to do car stuff.**

Roderick

Age 7

Daddy & Me

IN WHAT WAYS WOULD YOU LIKE TO BE LIKE YOUR DAD?

**In what way would I like to be like my daddy?
Why? Because he's so big and strong.
We ride the horse, play with the yellow ball
and I roll my hands.**

Mikaela

Age 2 ½

Daddy & Me

IN WHAT WAYS WOULD YOU LIKE TO BE LIKE YOUR DAD?

**I want to be like my dad
because he has a fun job.**

Kiel

Age 10

Daddy & Me

IN WHAT WAYS WOULD YOU LIKE TO BE LIKE YOUR DAD?

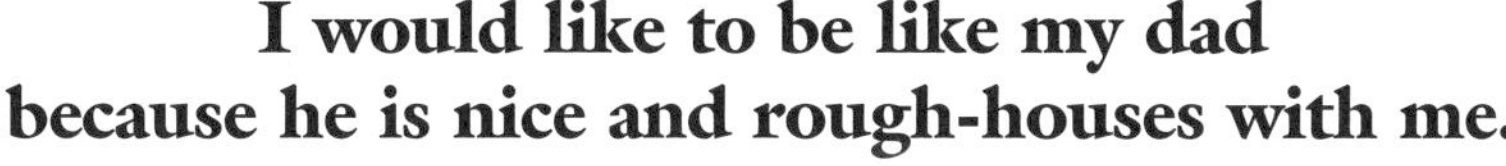

**I would like to be like my dad
because he is nice and rough-houses with me.**

Will

Age 10

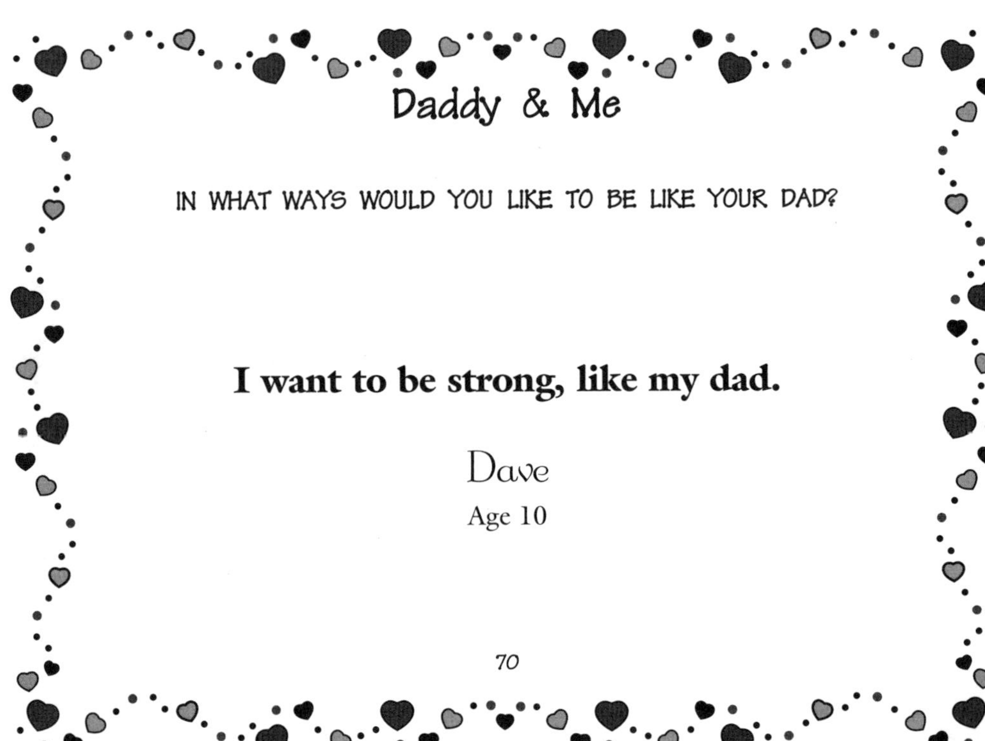

Daddy & Me

IN WHAT WAYS WOULD YOU LIKE TO BE LIKE YOUR DAD?

I want to be strong, like my dad.

Dave

Age 10

Daddy & Me

**I want to be smart, like my dad so
I can teach my children computers and drawing.
I also want to ride a motorcycle, just like my dad.**

Camille

Age 12

Daddy & Me

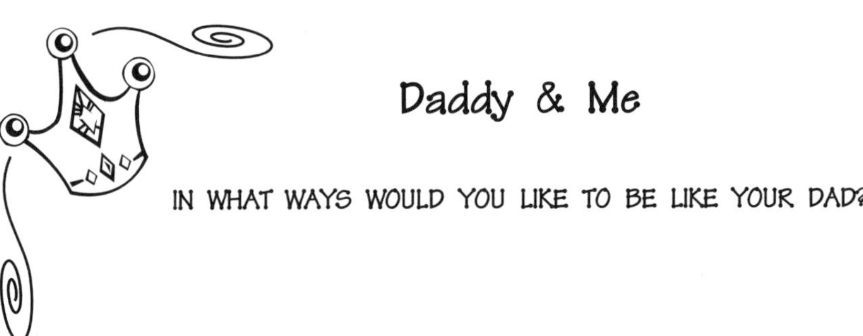

I want to be good, like my dad is.

Joey
Age 6

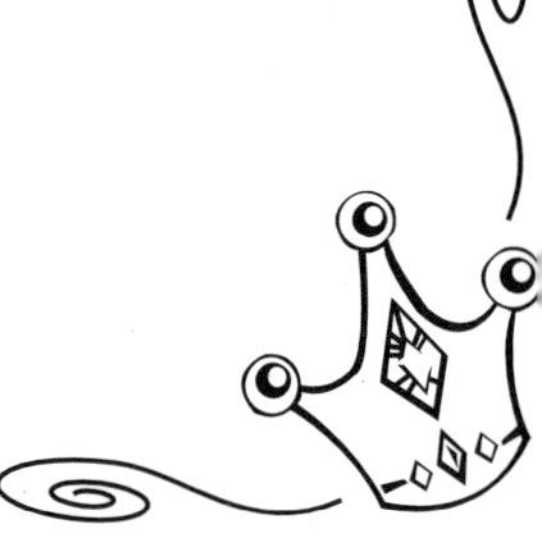

Daddy & Me

I would like to be like my father because he is cool.

Jim

Age 10

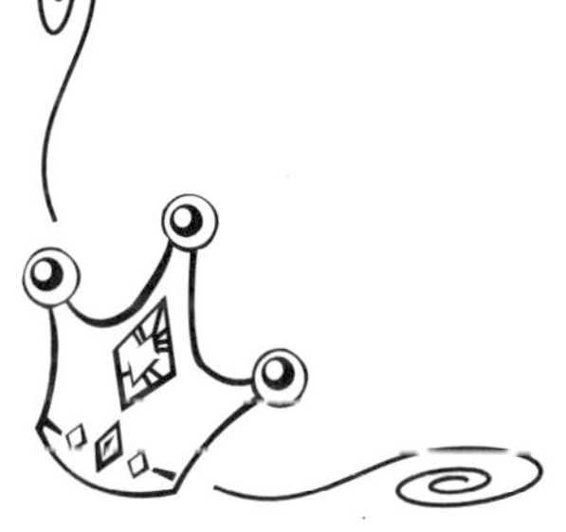

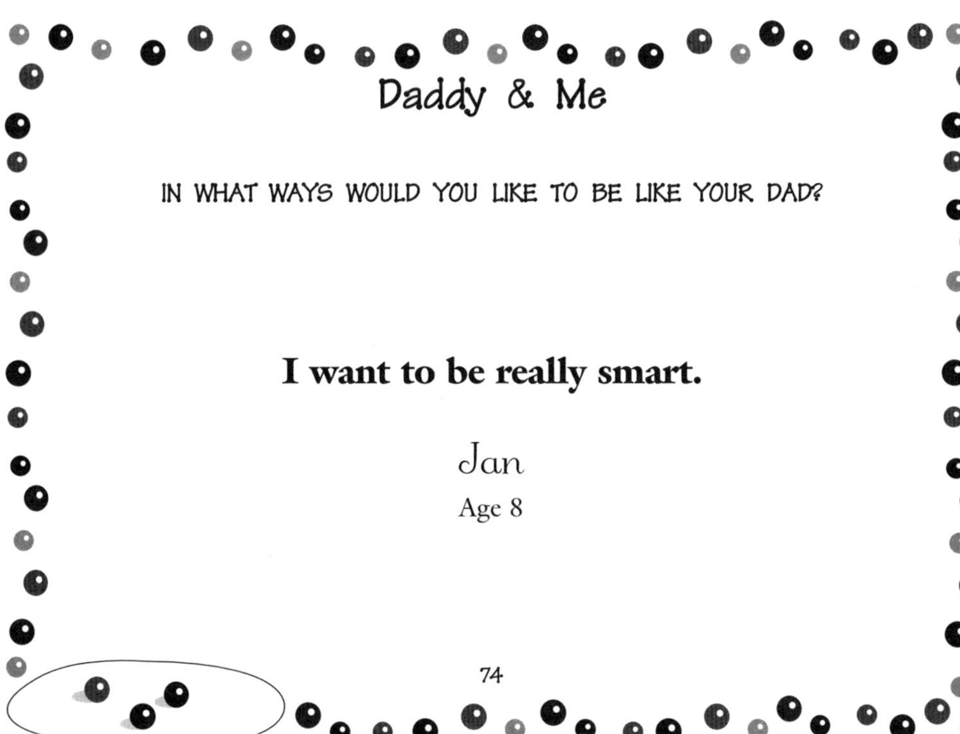

Daddy & Me

IN WHAT WAYS WOULD YOU LIKE TO BE LIKE YOUR DAD?

I want to be really smart.

Jan

Age 8

Daddy & Me

IN WHAT WAYS WOULD YOU LIKE TO BE LIKE YOUR DAD?

He is really strong and he can pick up anything.

Travis

Age 7

Daddy & Me

WHAT DO YOU LIKE MOST ABOUT YOUR FATHER?

He always thinks of me.

Vanessa

Age 10

Daddy & Me

WHAT DO YOU LIKE MOST ABOUT YOUR FATHER?

**The thing I like most about my dad
is he always plays Super Nintendo
with me and my brother.**

Jessica

Age 10

Daddy & Me

WHAT DO YOU LIKE MOST ABOUT YOUR FATHER?

He tells me I'm pretty.

Sheilagh

Age 6

Daddy & Me

WHAT DO YOU LIKE MOST ABOUT YOUR FATHER?

My dad is very funny and nice.

Jacque
Age 10

Daddy & Me

WHAT DO YOU LIKE MOST ABOUT YOUR FATHER?

My dad takes me camping.

Brent
Age 12

Daddy & Me

WHAT DO YOU LIKE MOST ABOUT YOUR FATHER?

My dad tries to get Blackhawks tickets for me and him.

Nick

Age 10

WHAT DO YOU LIKE MOST ABOUT YOUR FATHER?

Sometimes he lets me pretend I am driving.

Sheilagh
Age 6

Daddy & Me

WHAT DO YOU LIKE MOST ABOUT YOUR FATHER?

He got me a puppy for my birthday.

Carolyn

Age 8

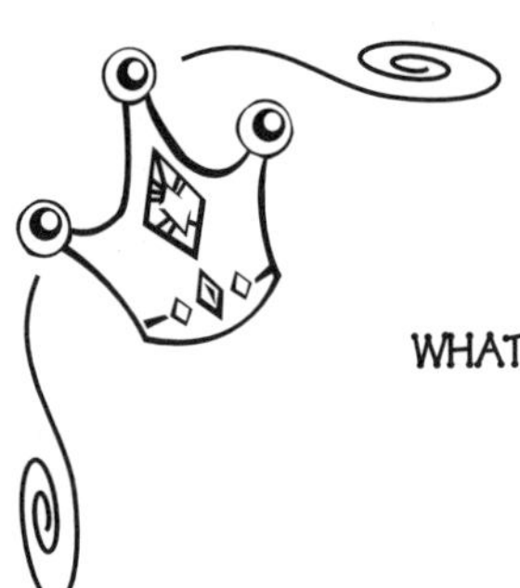

Daddy & Me

I like him because he is smart.

Dan

Age 10

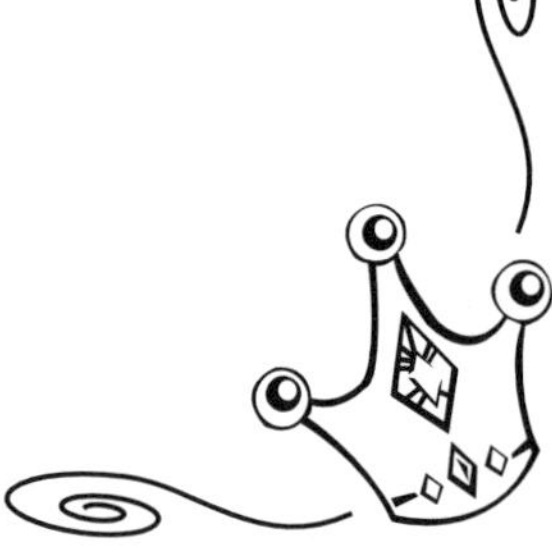

Daddy & Me

He always likes to do family things.

Jamie

Age 10

Daddy & Me

WHAT DO YOU LIKE MOST ABOUT YOUR FATHER?

My dad buys hot dogs and candy.

Jean

Age 4

Daddy & Me

WHAT DO YOU LIKE MOST ABOUT YOUR FATHER?

My dad has a stomach of steel.

Lori

Age 10

Daddy & Me

WHAT DO YOU LIKE MOST ABOUT YOUR FATHER?

My dad has a boat and it is fun.

Roderick

Age 7

Daddy & Me

WHAT DO YOU LIKE MOST ABOUT YOUR FATHER?

He spends time with me.

Caitlin

Age 10

Daddy & Me

I like the way my father makes me laugh when I don't feel good.

Eileen

Age 9

Daddy & Me

WHAT DO YOU LIKE MOST ABOUT YOUR FATHER?

He brings money home, for needs.

Cathy
Age 10

Daddy & Me

WHAT DO YOU LIKE MOST ABOUT YOUR FATHER?

He loves me and my mom.

Mark
Age 7

Daddy & Me

**My dad is always there for me
when I need him.**

Brent

Age 12

Daddy & Me

WHAT DO YOU LIKE MOST ABOUT YOUR FATHER?

He lets me help him when we fix things.

Matthew

Age 8

Daddy & Me

WHAT DO YOU LIKE MOST ABOUT YOUR FATHER?

He likes fishing.

Kiel

Age 10

Daddy & Me

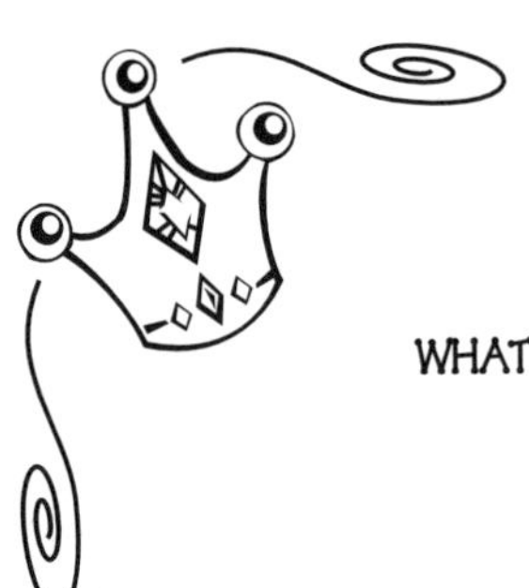

WHAT DO YOU LIKE MOST ABOUT YOUR FATHER?

I like it when we play catch.

Mark
Age 7

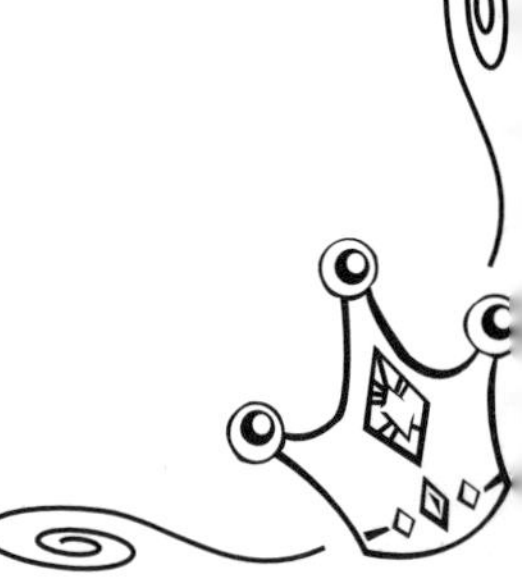

Daddy & Me

WHAT DO YOU LIKE MOST ABOUT YOUR FATHER?

He takes me places and does things with me.

Will

Age 10

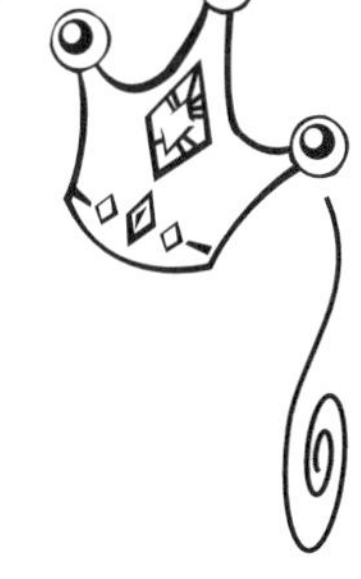

Daddy & Me

WHAT DO YOU LIKE MOST ABOUT YOUR FATHER?

He helps me with homework.

Dave

Age 10

Daddy & Me

I like the way my father calls me "friend".

Pat

Age 9

Daddy & Me

WHAT DO YOU LIKE MOST ABOUT YOUR FATHER?

**He tries the best that he can
to get me where I'm going.**

Jim

Age 10

Daddy & Me

WHAT DO YOU LIKE MOST ABOUT YOUR FATHER?

**He helps me whenever
I need help with things.**

Jamie

Age 10

Daddy & Me

He lets me wear his shirts and ties.

Camille

Age 12

Daddy & Me

WHAT DO YOU LIKE MOST ABOUT YOUR FATHER?

He works hard
and he buys my mom pretty things.

Jan

Age 8

Daddy & Me

WHAT DO YOU LIKE MOST ABOUT YOUR FATHER?

My dad makes cookies every Christmas.

Travis

Age 8

Daddy & Me

I LOVE MY DAD SO MUCH THAT I WOULD.....

-try never to disappoint him!

Ginger

Age 11

Daddy & Me

I LOVE MY DAD SO MUCH THAT I WOULD.....

-stick up for him,
if someone makes fun of him.

Melissa

Age 12

Daddy & Me

I LOVE MY DAD SO MUCH THAT I WOULD......

-that I would give him a kiss!

Vicki

Age 6

Daddy & Me

I LOVE MY DAD SO MUCH THAT I WOULD.....

I would die for him.

April

Age 12

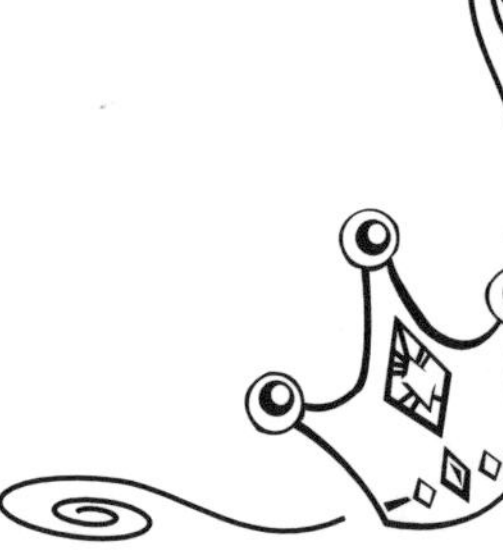

Daddy & Me

I LOVE MY DAD SO MUCH THAT I WOULD.....

-clean the garage.

Tim

Age 11

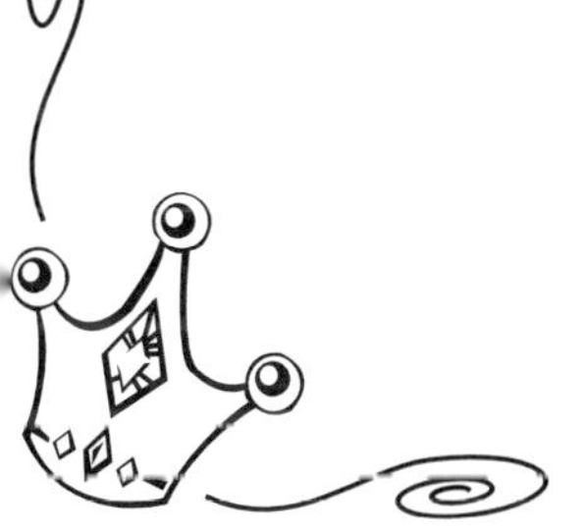

Daddy & Me

I LOVE MY DAD SO MUCH THAT I WOULD.....

**-give him a big hug and kiss
when he comes home from work.**

Nicole

Age 5

Daddy & Me

I LOVE MY DAD SO MUCH THAT I WOULD.....

Always tell the truth.

Travis

Age 8

Daddy & Me

I LOVE MY DAD SO MUCH THAT I WOULD.....

always do what he asks.

Sean

Age 8 ½

Daddy & Me

I LOVE MY DAD SO MUCH THAT I WOULD.....

-play (with him).

Mikaela

Age 2 ½

Daddy & Me

I LOVE MY DAD SO MUCH THAT I WOULD.....

-hug him.

Joey
Age 6

Daddy & Me

-care about him and love him forever.

Mary

Age 5

Daddy & Me

I LOVE MY DAD SO MUCH THAT I WOULD.....

-hug and kiss him.

Aaron

Age 10

Daddy & Me

I LOVE MY DAD SO MUCH THAT I WOULD.....

Help him clean the garage on Saturdays.

Jan

Age 8

Daddy & Me

I LOVE MY DAD SO MUCH THAT I WOULD.....

Help him with his homework.

Sheilagh

Age 6

Daddy & Me

I LOVE MY DAD SO MUCH THAT I WOULD.....

KISS HIM!

Jenny
Age 5

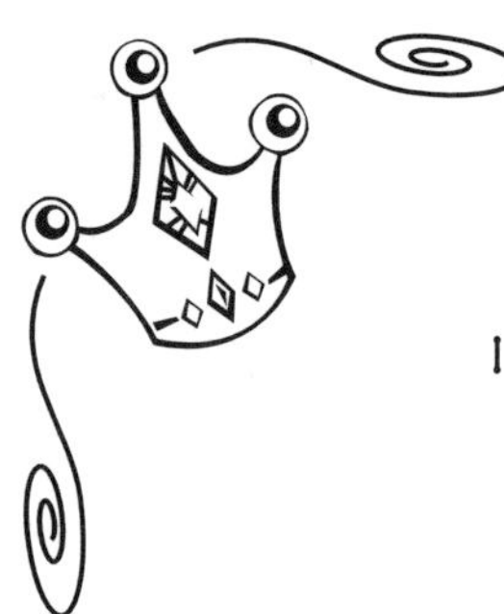

Daddy & Me

I LOVE MY DAD SO MUCH THAT I WOULD.....

-like to give him a gift.

Rachelle

Age 6

Daddy & Me

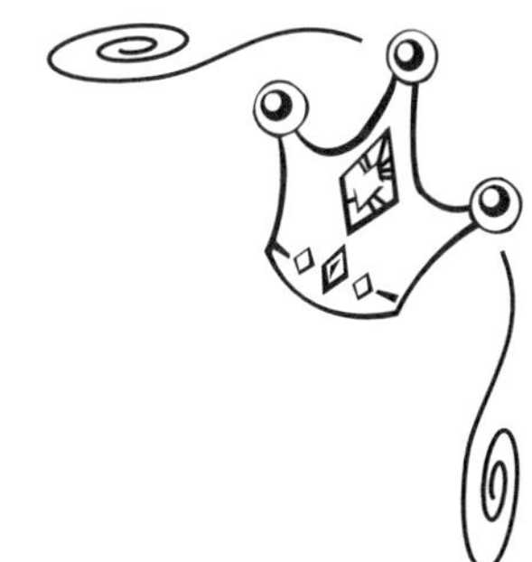

MY DAD IS THE BEST BECAUSE.....

-he is very polite and listens to what I say.

Ginger

Age 11

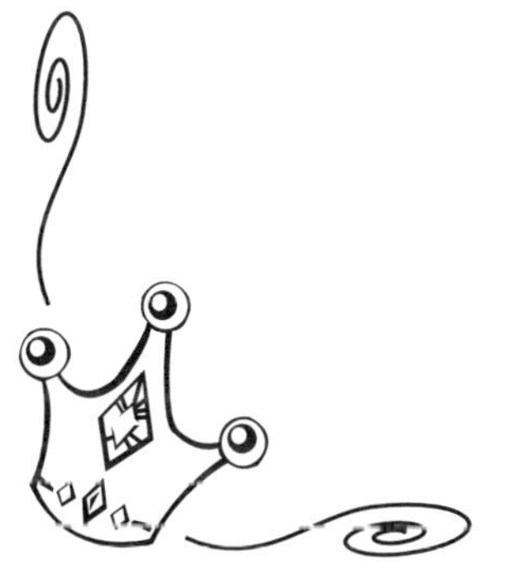

Daddy & Me

MY DAD IS THE BEST BECAUSE......

-he bought me a bike with his bonus money.

Camille

Age 12

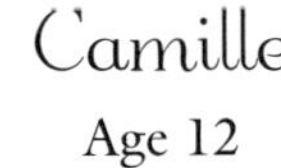

Daddy & Me

-he doesn't make me put on the worms when we go fish.

Molly

Age 6

Daddy & Me

MY DAD IS THE BEST BECAUSE......

-he cares about me and loves me.

Melissa

Age 12

Daddy & Me

MY DAD IS THE BEST BECAUSE......

-he takes me for pancakes.

Sarah

Age 3

Daddy & Me

MY DAD IS THE BEST BECAUSE.....

He comes with me to baseball and helps us.

Tim

Age 11

Daddy & Me

MY DAD IS THE BEST BECAUSE.....

-he loves me.

Vicki

Age 6

Daddy & Me

MY DAD IS THE BEST BECAUSE......

-he doesn't let my brothers pick on me.

Pat

Age 9

Daddy & Me

MY DAD IS THE BEST BECAUSE......

-he always has time for me.

Brent
Age 12

Daddy & Me

MY DAD IS THE BEST BECAUSE......

-he loves me so much.

Nicole

Age 5

Daddy & Me

MY DAD IS THE BEST BECAUSE......

-he's my dad and I love him.

Dave
Age 13

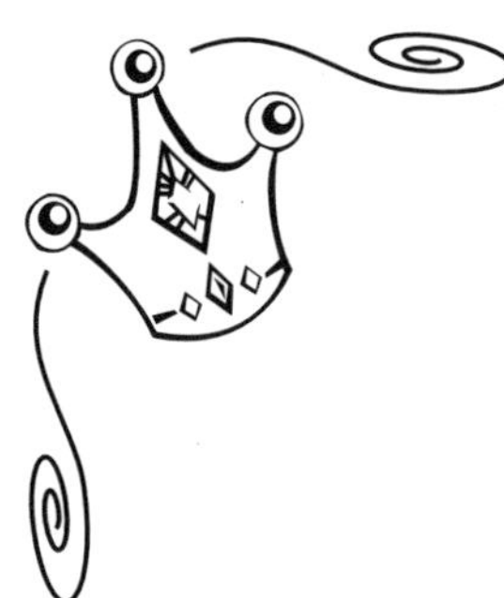

Daddy & Me

MY DAD IS THE BEST BECAUSE......

-he cares for me.

Sean

Age 8 ½

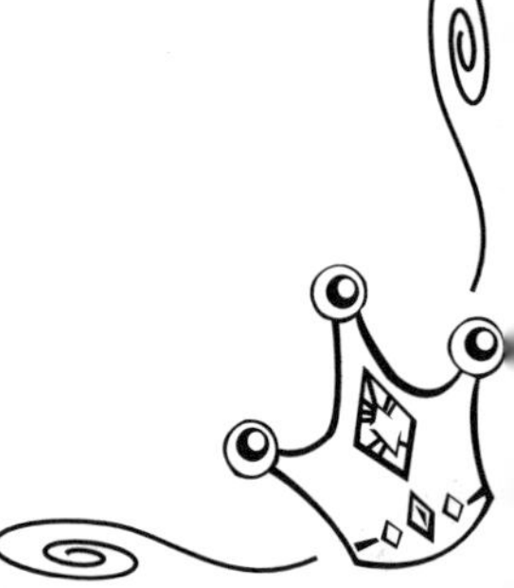

Daddy & Me

MY DAD IS THE BEST BECAUSE.....

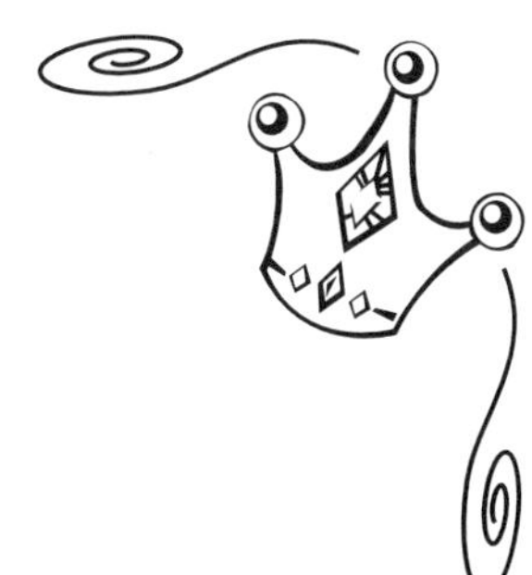

-he's my best friend.

Mikaela

Age 2 ½

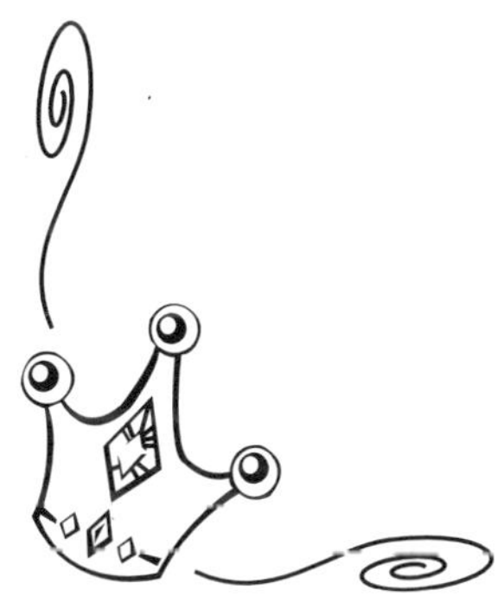

Daddy & Me

MY DAD IS THE BEST BECAUSE......

-he cares for me.

Joey

Age 6

Daddy & Me

MY DAD IS THE BEST BECAUSE......

-he loves me and cares about me.

Mary

Age 5

Daddy & Me

MY DAD IS THE BEST BECAUSE......

-he is very loving and kind.

Aaron

Age 10

Daddy & Me

MY DAD IS THE BEST BECAUSE.....

**-he painted a hop scotch
at our house to play.**

Katie

Age 9

Daddy & Me

MY DAD IS THE BEST BECAUSE......

**-because he does so many
wonderful things for me.**

Jan

Age 8

138

Daddy & Me

MY DAD IS THE BEST BECAUSE.....

-he can pick me up.

Jenny

Age 5

Daddy & Me

MY DAD IS THE BEST BECAUSE......

-he can fix anything.

Rachelle

Age 6

Daddy & Me

MY DAD IS THE BEST BECAUSE......

-he makes my mom happy.

Joe

Age 8

Daddy & Me

**-the thing I like to do with my dad
is going ice skating with him and my brother.**

Jessica

Age 10

Daddy & Me

WHAT DO YOU LIKE TO DO WITH YOUR FATHER?

-I like to watch TV and tell jokes with him.
I also like to play basketball with him.

Jacque
Age 10

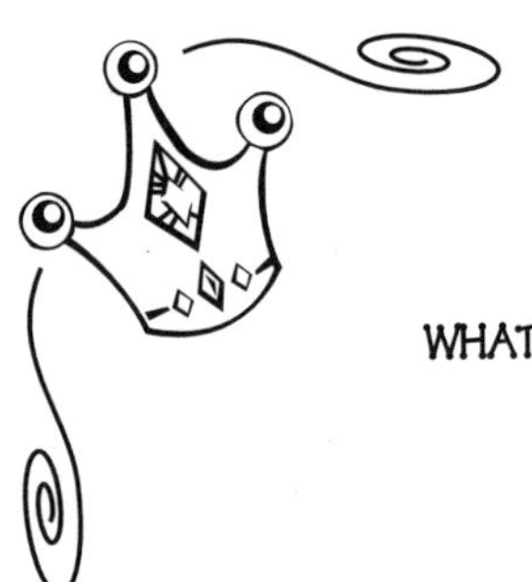

Daddy & Me

WHAT DO YOU LIKE TO DO WITH YOUR FATHER?

-PLAY BASEBALL!

Nick

Age 10

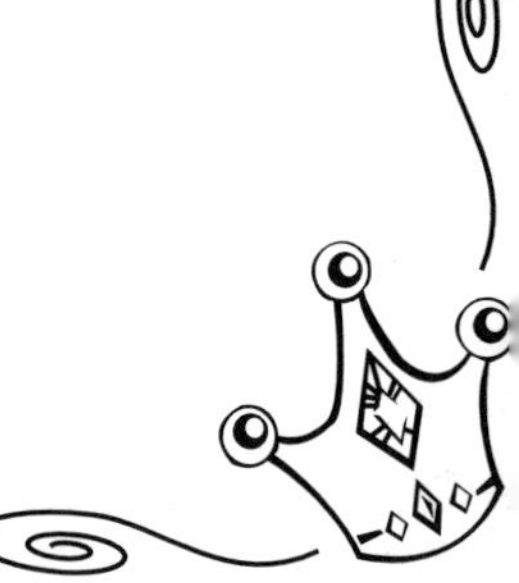

Daddy & Me

We read the comics.

Travis

Age 8

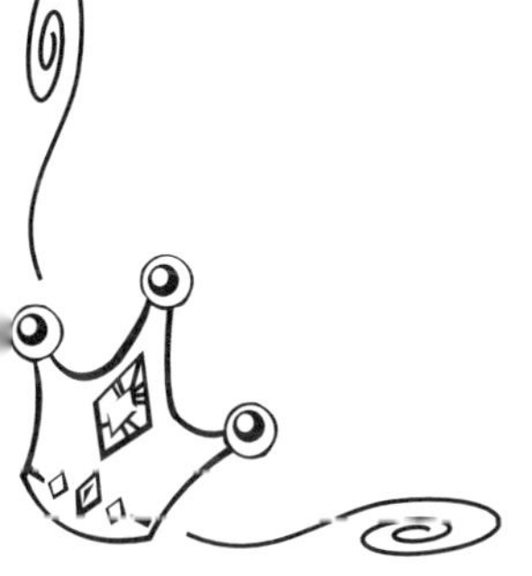

Daddy & Me

WHAT DO YOU LIKE TO DO WITH YOUR FATHER?

-I like to do special things.

Jamie

Age 10

Daddy & Me

WHAT DO YOU LIKE TO DO WITH YOUR FATHER?

-play catch with my dad.

Kelly
Age 10

Daddy & Me

WHAT DO YOU LIKE TO DO WITH YOUR FATHER?

-watch car races with him.

Lori

Age 10

Daddy & Me

WHAT DO YOU LIKE TO DO WITH YOUR FATHER?

-go to stores, (EVERYTHING).

Caitlin

Age 10

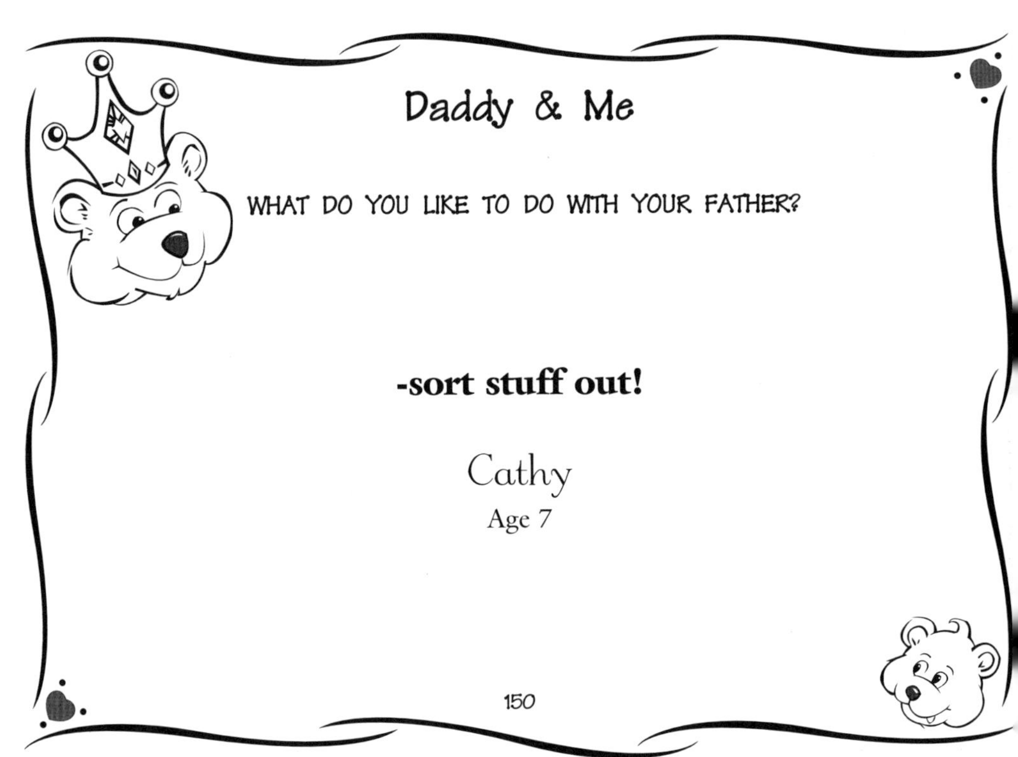

Daddy & Me

WHAT DO YOU LIKE TO DO WITH YOUR FATHER?

-sort stuff out!

Cathy
Age 7

Daddy & Me

WHAT DO YOU LIKE TO DO WITH YOUR FATHER?

-go fishing with him.

Kiel

Age 10

Daddy & Me

WHAT DO YOU LIKE TO DO WITH YOUR FATHER?

-I like to do the computer with daddy.

Sarah

Age 3

Daddy & Me

WHAT DO YOU LIKE TO DO WITH YOUR FATHER?

-go sledding with my dad and fishing.

Will

Age 10

Daddy & Me

WHAT DO YOU LIKE TO DO WITH YOUR FATHER?

-practice soccer and go places with him.

Allison

Age 10

Daddy & Me

WHAT DO YOU LIKE TO DO WITH YOUR FATHER?

**-I like to help him with things
and go places with him.**

Roderick

Age 7

Daddy & Me

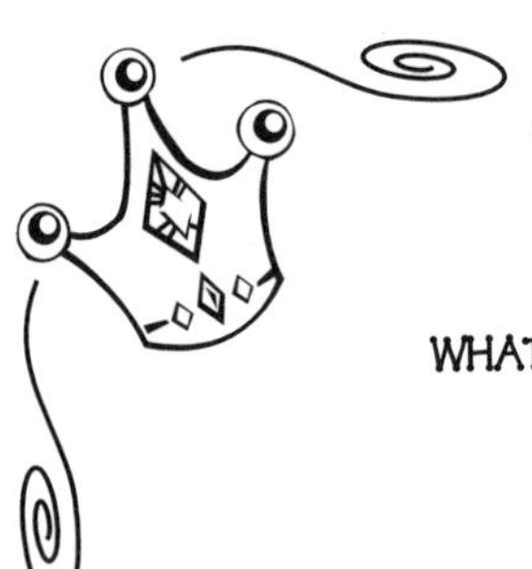

WHAT DO YOU LIKE TO DO WITH YOUR FATHER?

-I just like to be with my dad because I want to be like my dad.

Ashish

Age 9

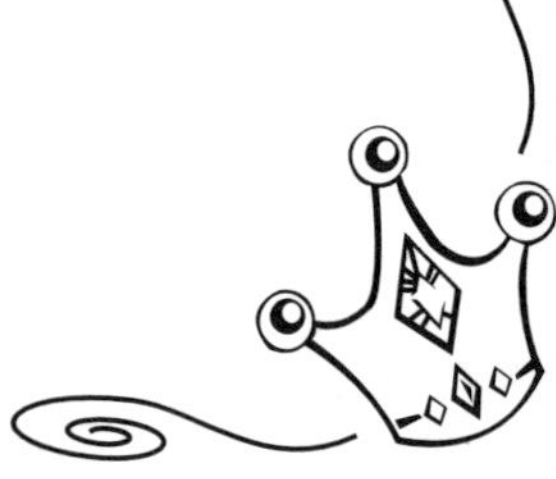

Daddy & Me

WHAT DO YOU LIKE TO DO WITH YOUR FATHER?

-I like him to carry me.

Jean

Age 4

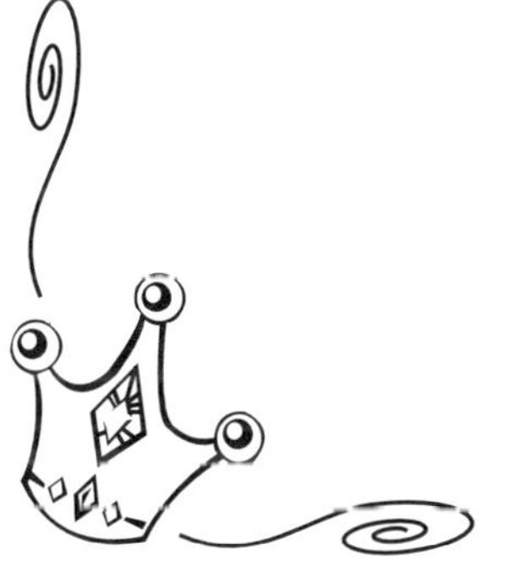

Daddy & Me

WHAT DO YOU LIKE TO DO WITH YOUR FATHER?

**-I like to do nice things
for my mom with my dad.**

Carolyn

Age 8

Daddy & Me

WHAT DO YOU LIKE TO DO WITH YOUR FATHER?

-make breakfast for my mom.

Jan

Age 8

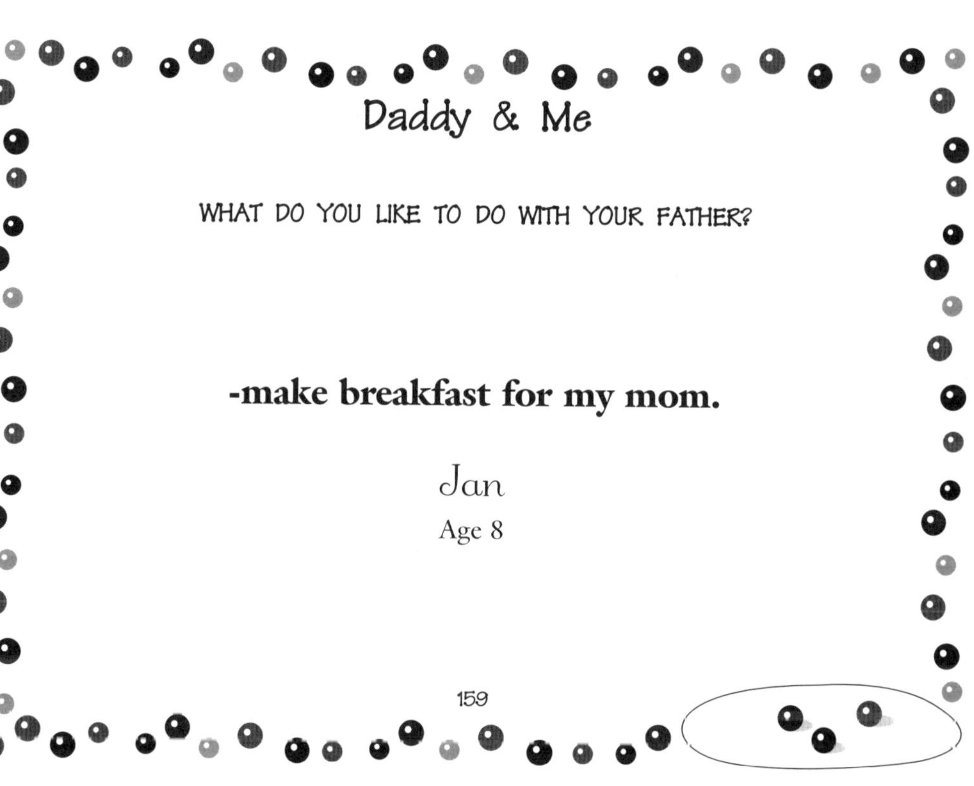

Daddy & Me

WHAT DO YOU LIKE TO DO WITH YOUR FATHER?

-helping him with yard work.

Dave
Age 10

Daddy & Me

WHAT DO YOU LIKE TO DO WITH YOUR FATHER?

-we fix his car on the weekends.

Matthew

Age 8

Daddy & Me

WHAT DO YOU LIKE TO DO WITH YOUR FATHER?

-we go to visit my big brother at the fire station and get to see the fire trucks.

Tim

Age 11

Daddy & Me

-I like to go to hockey games with my dad.

Jim

Age 10

Daddy & Me

WHAT DO YOU LIKE TO DO WITH YOUR FATHER?

-I like to build things.

Jamie

Age 10

Daddy & Me

WHAT DO YOU LIKE TO DO WITH YOUR FATHER?

**-My dad and me get to plant flowers
at our house.**

Sheilagh

Age 6

Daddy & Me

-I like using tools to cut things.

Mark

Age 7

Daddy & Me

WHAT DO YOU LIKE TO DO WITH YOUR FATHER?

-go to a skating rink and skate with him.

Vanessa

Age 10

Other Titles by Great Quotations

201 Best Things Ever Said
The ABC's of Parenting
African-American Wisdom
As A Cat Thinketh
The Best of Friends
The Birthday Astrologer
Chicken Soup
The Cornerstones of Success
Daddy & Me
Fantastic Father, Dependable Dad
For Mother, A Bouquet of Sentiments
Global Wisdom
Golden Years, Golden Words
Grandma, I Love You
Growing Up in Toyland
Happiness Is Found Along the Way
Hollywords
Hooked on Golf
In Celebration of Women
Inspirations
Interior Design for Idiots
I'm Not Over the Hill
The Lemonade Handbook
Let's Talk Decorating
Life's Lessons
Life's Simple Pleasures
A Lifetime of Love
A Light Heart Lives Long

Midwest Wisdom
Mommy & Me
Mrs. Aesop's Fables
Mother, I Love You
Motivating Quotes for Motivated People
Mrs. Murphy's Laws
Mrs. Webster's Dictionary
My Daughter, My Special Friend
The Other Species
Parenting 101
The Perfect Man
Reflections
Romantic Rhapsody
The Rose Mystique
The Secret Language of Men
The Secret Language of Women
The Secrets in Your Name
Social Disgraces
Some Things Never Change
The Sports Page
Sports Widow
Stress or Sanity
A Teacher Is Better Than Two Books
TeenAge of Insanity
Thanks from the Heart
Things You'll Learn...
Wedding Wonders
Working Woman's World

GREAT QUOTATIONS PUBLISHING COMPANY

Glendale Heights, IL 60139
Phone (630) 582-2800 • Fax (630) 582-2813